MEGHAN SCHULTZ

Exhausted Mommy Beauty

Fast, frugal, and fabulous beauty and wellness tips for busy mamas that want to look and feel their best

This book is dedicated to my awesome mama, Patty Hart

"Being a mom has made me so tired. And so happy"

Tina Fey

Contents

1

Notes

The recommendations in this book are not to be used to treat, diagnose, cure, or prevent any disease or ailment. If you have any concerns, please consult your physician.

I mention several different skin care and makeup brands in this book. I'm not being paid or endorsed by these companies in any way. I'm only recommending products that I love!

2

Introduction

Hey mama. I see you.

You're exhausted. I get it.

If there are days you feel lucky enough to take a shower and put on real clothes, then this book is for you.

As a former pageant queen, and as a professional in the field of makeup and skincare, I've always had a love for beauty and fashion. When I entered the high calling of motherhood, the time and budget for the things I loved in these categories went immediately to the back burner. As I'm writing this introduction, I have my baby son on my lap. I've been awake since 11 PM since he fussed all night (it's now afternoon the following day), and I'm at a "zombie" level of exhaustion. If that isn't stressful enough, I'm writing this book in 2022, when inflation is at an all-time high.

Look nice? Hair done? Flawless makeup? Yeah, ok. Who's got the time or the money for that right now?

I totally get it.

But girl, I got you.

Can you be an excellent mama while still looking and feeling great? Yes!

Yes, there are days when I don't have makeup on, and I'm still wearing my breast milk-stained pajamas at 2 PM while trying to do the dishes from last night's dinner. It happens. Often.

So, before we go any further I want to remind you that you should give yourself some grace. Don't pressure yourself into the Instagram beauty standards of today. It's all smoke in mirrors. This book is simply a compilation of look good/feel good things I enjoy, and I want to help other women who enjoy those things too.

No pressure.

No impossible standards.

Just fun and helpful beauty hacks for tired mamas on a crunched time schedule and tight budget.

So without further adieu, let's get past this intro, because we don't have time nor the energy to dilly dally.

It's ok mama. You got this!

3

Self Care

I have to admit, I felt a little hypocritical as I started writing this chapter. This is probably the most important sections of the entire book, and yet I must constantly remind myself to do these self-care things on my own. I have self-care at the top of the list of this beauty book because without it, no matter how much concealer we put on, we won't feel beautiful. Let's face it mama, it's hard to take care of ourselves when we have littles and a spouse that need things too. My husband, God bless him, has to *really* crack down on me to stop and rest sometimes. As a wife and mother, instinctually, I usually don't. Feed the baby, change the baby, thaw the chicken for dinner tonight, throw a load of laundry in for work clothes tomorrow, do we have any eggs left in the fridge for breakfast in the morning? Ohmygosh, did I miss that doctor appointment? Yeesh.

As my husband constantly tells me (and I humbly admit he's right), if I don't take care of myself, I won't be able to properly care for our family. If I run myself into the ground to the point of being ill, that doesn't help anyone.

If you don't read any other chapter in the book, just read this one and remember: You must fill up your cup so you can pour into theirs. There is no virtue in purposefully allowing yourself to become so exhausted that you become physically, spiritually, and mentally unwell. Now granted, sometimes we don't have a choice. There will be days (or weeks) we're fatigued to the point of insanity, because running a household, working, and taking care of a family have their daily necessary demands. There is simply no way around it. I recall one evening (not too long ago) my husband taking our crying baby out of my arms and telling me to go to bed to get some rest, to which I replied "But I haven't eaten since breakfast, I'm starving. Just let me get some food first." I was able to scarf something down, but after nourishing myself, I couldn't crawl into bed, because it was time for crying baby to breastfeed again. You get my point.

As you take in these recommendations for self-care, give yourself some mercy. Don't feel bad if you can't prioritize all the self-care things every single day. Get what you can when you can. When you feel good, that beautiful energy emanates outward. You'll have a pep in your step, your face and skin will glow, and your smile will be bigger. And there's nothing more beautiful than a genuine smile.

Also remind yourself that it's ok to ask for help. As a people-pleaser, it's VERY hard for me to ask for help as I hate the idea of inconveniencing anyone. Girl. ASK. FOR. HELP. You have to. You were never designed to take this whole motherhood journey alone. So next time you find yourself on your 3rd day of dry shampoo, and frazzled to the point of maniacal laughter, try to implement as least ONE of these basic self-care necessities.

1.) **Read the Bible, pray, and practice gratitude**. If there is any habit you try to implement daily, make it this one. Even if all you have is 30 seconds (as mothers, we know there are days when we literally have only 30 seconds), read a Bible verse and silently say "Thank you, Jesus, for this beautiful sunny day", or "Thank you, God, for the roof over my head". You don't have to make it overly complex. Get one of those Bible apps that can text you a verse of the day, and thank God for something in your life. Anything. The fascinating thing about gratitude is that it is that research shows it is impossible for anxiety and gratitude to co-exist in the brain at the same time. Impossible! Isn't that wild? So next time you are feeling crippled with all the normal worries a mama has to deal with every day, switch that brain over to something that you are thankful for, and do it continuously.

Also, don't forget to come to God with your problems. Placing your worries and issues into the hands of an omniscient, loving Father, and allowing Him to take care of things in your life will be a huge relief mentally and spiritually.

Prayer is powerful, and it works. Try it out.

2.) **Don't forget about basic hygiene**. It's incredible what you forget (or choose not to do) when all you've only had a few hours of sleep over the course of several days. That was me as a new mommy. That first week was a blur of exhaustion I've never known as I was sleeping only 45 minutes a night. Between the pain of labor, the anxiety of motherhood, and spending hours trying to breastfeed a screaming baby that didn't latch, all the days ran together. I had to really think hard about the last time I had showered or brushed my teeth. Thankfully, my visiting family was able to hold the baby while I took care of myself for 30 minutes in those first few weeks. It got harder when the family wasn't there anymore, and real life began. When you are home alone with a little one, it can be tough to squeeze the necessities in. Some people may call me crazy, but even if I've only had a few hours of sleep, I try to get up before the little one wakes so I can take care of myself. Sometimes I choose sleep over these necessities, but I've found that if I can have a little morning routine of a shower, a little makeup and some real clothes, I feel a million times better. If I'm feeling really froggy, I may even shave my legs. This basic self-care gives me a sense of normalcy, and a sense accomplishment. Mentally and emotionally, it helps me get ready for a busy day when I feel better and look like I have myself put together.

3.) **Get some exercise and sunshine.** Ah, yes, that whole 20-30 minutes of exercise, blah blah blah. We all know we should, but executing this task as a mama can be daunting. The very thought of *any* exercise after a night of only 3 hours of sleep with a fussy baby makes me scoff, "HA! Yeah, no". But girl, we gotta. The benefits of even a few minutes of exercise and/or sunshine are astronomical. Once again, don't turn this into something overly complex, and get that silly idea of an Instagramable bikini beach body out of your head. Focus on health because heath is beautiful. If all you can do is a five-minute walk down the street and back, do it. Often, my level of fatigue is so intense that the thought of struggling with a stroller or one of those hold-the-baby-body-wrappy-things is just too overwhelming, so I simply take the baby in my arms, and walk down my road. 5 minutes. Exercise. Sunshine. Done. Do what you can and build from there. Just a few minutes to get that blood flowing will bring a freshness to your body and mind. Also, don't discredit all the physical labor you do during the day as a mama. Do you feel those strong biceps forming from holding a 10+ lb. baby for hours on end? Yeah, that definitely counts!

4.) **Sleep**. I imagine you probably saw the title of this book and picked it up because you, like me, are severely sleep deprived, as most mamas are. As I'm the current mama of a newborn, sleep is precious and scarce.

The first step toward a beautiful, healthy body and mind is sleep. Sleep is vital. It helps us fight off illness, wards off depression, builds our immune system, and ramps up our metabolism. Your skin and eye area will immediately let you know if sleep is something that's lacking in your life. Sleep is literally the reset and recharge button for our body. It will help you look and feel top-notch. You've probably heard people say, "sleep when the baby sleeps". This advice is valuable as it is frustrating. I want to use baby's nap time to catch up on everything else I've been neglecting. In a moment like that, I just have to recall the wise words of my dearest Aunt Peggy. When dishes are piled high, and that huge load of laundry is still sitting on the living room couch, she would take one look around, and with an adorable upper-octave giggle she'd shrug and say, "Oh well!". Because of that two-word phrase, I've learned to throw perfection out the window, and allowed myself the grace to prioritize accordingly. Take the nap, girl. Just take the nap. If all you have is the opportunity to sleep for 15-20 minutes, do it! I wrestle with the idea that such a little window of sleep doesn't help anything, but I assure you, it does, and there is scientific research to back it up. Just like exercise, get what you can, when you can. Your skin, hair, nails, body, and mind will thank you.

5.) **Eat nutritious, healthy food**. Healthy food is essential for a properly functioning body and is the epitome of self-care. I could go on for hours about this subject, but that will be another book for another day. Healthy food is the foundation of beauty and good energy. Fruits and vegetables bring life to your body's cells, which are the building blocks for lovely skin, hair, nails, etc. You should also take note of is how your body reacts when you eat certain foods. Do you have an acne breakout if you eat dairy? Does your skin look inflamed if you eat gluten? Pay attention to every detail that your body is trying to communicate with you. I know it's hard not to crave the bad things – especially when we are tired. Junk food is very pleasurable and comforting. Add pregnancy or breastfeeding cravings into the mix and you have a perfect storm for eating half a box of Little Debbie's at 3 AM. If cravings weren't hard enough to deal with, having the time and energy to purchase and food prep healthy meals can feel overwhelming. If you are frequently up in the middle of the night with baby, try to keep quick wholesome foods in the fridge that can satisfy you immediately. A handful of grapes, or antioxidant rich berries are easy, tasty, and nutritious (no pre-cutting required!). During the day, if you are craving something naughty, make smoothies! It can be as easy as throwing pre-mixed frozen berries, with water and ice into a blender. It's perfect for consuming on the go, or one handed while holding baby. Choosing healthy foods will create a healthy glow, even if you are an exhausted mommy. Also, a little caffeine doesn't hurt.

6.) **Have a tribe**. We as humans were not designed to function alone. Find a group of like-minded women you enjoy connecting with. Mommy support groups, bible studies, church, local community groups, clubs, close friends etc. I'm not just talking about Facebook groups (although that can be a good place to start). I'm talking about physical, face-to-face fellowship with other genuine and positive ladies. This is crucial for your emotional, spiritual, and mental health.

7.) **Have a goal**. To put it simply, a woman filled with hope and happiness shines. Proverbs 29:18 says, "Where there is no vision, the people perish". Make sure that you have a goal to shoot for, or something to look forward to. It could be as simple as working on a house project, saving up for a vacation, or even earning your degree. I personally, always need to have some type of goal or project in front of me. If I don't, I start to flounder and feel depressed, and my face will begin to show it. Every day feels the same, and I develop a negative outlook on life. When the baby is sleeping (if I'm not taking a nap), I'm usually working on a project. For me, it's working on my business side hustles, designing something, or learning something new. Working on this book was one of those projects. It gives you something exciting to strive for, and it gives oneself a tremendous sense of accomplishment. Ambitions give life to an exhausted human.

Have a goal, then get it, girl.

4

Essential Facial Skin Care

Everyone is unique, and there are hundreds of different skin types out there, so in this chapter I'm going to cover basic skin care and remedies that most mamas need. If you are having a severe issue that you can't seem to figure out, make sure to see your dermatologist.

Facial skin care is essential because it is the canvas on which your makeup rests. Ideally, the better your skin, the less makeup you'll need. When I went to Paris with my husband several year ago, I noticed the amazing beauty routines that French women implement into their daily lifestyle. After cleansing, a French woman's beauty regimen will usually consist of a toner, moisturizer, eye cream, serum, sunscreen, and lipstick. Here in the United States, American women will usually put on moisturizer, primer, foundation, concealer, blush, highlighter, 5 different eyeshadow colors, mascara, eyebrow filler, lipstick, and lip gloss. See the difference? I think we could learn a thing or two from our lovely French sisters that put more of an emphasis on skin care and natural beauty. Now don't get me wrong, I LOVE makeup. I'm guilty of using many makeup products daily, but I've also learned to care for my skin a little more. In addition, I'm learning to free myself of the idea that I need to cover everything up.

Let your natural beauty shine through!

I know what you're thinking. Sounds great, but what mama has the time or the cash for a luxurious skin care routine?

Girl, I got you.

We are going to go over some amazing skin care tips that's both fast and frugal for frazzled mamas!

Start with cleansing. Make sure to get a cleanser specifically your skin type. The skin on your face is different than the skin on your body, so its best to find a gentle cleanser specifically for the face. Body soaps can sometimes be too drying or harsh for the delicate skin from the neck upward. If you have oily skin, look for something specifically designed for oily skin and not something that ads moisture etc. In addition to skin type, I always encourage cleansers that are naturally derived, organic, or free of harsh chemicals or toxins. Brands like Burts Bees, Native, Juice Beauty, Avalon Organics and Young Living meet most if not all these criteria. Cleansers with exfoliators are even better, as they take off that dull top layer of skin cells revealing the new fresh skin cells underneath. The exfoliation process also makes fine lines less prominent and brings blood flow to the face resulting in a fresh glow. This can be particularly helpful when you are sleep deprived. When we are exhausted, our breathing gets shallow. This means blood and oxygen are not going to all the necessary parts of the body the way it should, resulting in dull, pale, or discolored skin. A rigorous scrub is literal CPR to a tired face.

I'm a firm believer in the wash twice method. This is mostly for nighttime when you have all that oil, gunk, and makeup on. Wash once to remove the makeup, then wash again to clean deeper into your pores. If you wash only once, you are literally smearing the makeup all over the surface of your face, and your pores may remain clogged with oil and makeup. I recommend using some type of foaming cleanser or oil specifically designed to dissolve makeup, followed by an electric exfoliating brush with liquid face soap. If you don't want to mess with any fancy equipment, a simple homemade sugar scrub from Pinterest does wonders.

If you're already like, "Girl, I ain't got time for that", fear not! Bare minimum, just get a simple face cleanser and wash your face twice. Ones with a pump dispenser that you can keep in the shower save even more time. Don't worry about exfoliating every day. Depending on your skin, you can usually get away with a once-a-week exfoliation.

After cleansing, you may want to use a toner. To be honest, I find this step to be optional. It's not gonna make a huge difference if you skip it. Toners serve the purpose of minimizing pores, tightening the skin, and restoring a hydration balance, so it definitely has its perks if you choose to involve this step in your skin care. Usually, toners are applied with a cotton ball, but I find the spray on toners to be much faster and more convenient. As a time crunched mama, not having to fumble for a cotton ball can save a few precious seconds in the morning, and those few seconds here and there really add up.

Added bonus with spray on toner: If you've already had your makeup on for 12 hours and you still have somewhere to be, spritz a little on over your makeup to give yourself that dewy, freshly applied makeup look. (Plus, a little cold spritz to the face will help wake you up!)

Serums. Now we gettin' fancy. These are the luxurious magic potions of the skin care world. Serums are lightweight liquids that are highly concentrated to target specific skin issues. Because these products are so concentrated, only a few drops are needed in most cases. If you purchase a high-quality product, you'll see some really cool results rather quickly. If your skin is screaming for help, this may be a good place to start. Serums are not moisturizers, so you'll need some hydration in addition to a serum if your skin is dry. There are thousands of serums on the market today, so my requirement for finding a good one is to focus on a specific skin concern. Is it hyperpigmentation (acne scaring/sun damage)? Fine lines? Dullness? For exhausted mamas, I recommend something for brightening dull, tired skin. Products with vitamin C or fruit extract will usually accomplish this. If you are overwhelmed on where to start looking for a good serum, I always suggest brands such as Clinique, Rodan & Fields, Juice Beauty, and Strivectin. I can personally attest that these are fantastic product lines that will give wonderful results.

Eye cream. Oh, girl. We mamas NEED eye cream. When my baby sings the operatic song of his people from midnight to 5 AM, this is one skin care step I cannot go without. I apply some every morning to help with dark circles and puffiness while drinking a caffeinated beverage. Eye products that include cooling roller balls can be helpful as well (cold helps reduce swelling aka. eye bags). This may sound trite, but a couple cucumber slices out of the fridge applied to the eyes can help reduce swelling as well. Even if you don't get great results, at least my millennial sisters can feel like Mia Thermopolis for a few minutes. Another antidote and time saver for distraught eye areas are these little things called eye masks. Oh man, this invention is so helpful and time saving! Simply stick them on, go to your kitchen for some coffee, change a diaper, then peel them off and toss! How easy is that? This may be the newest and most amazing skin care staple for every mama out there today.

Next, we have moisturizers. If you have super oily skin, you may not need to include this step in your skin care routine. The great thing about moisturizers is that most of them on the market are 3 steps in one (moisturizer, serum, and SPF). So not only are you moisturizing, you're also taking care of skin issues while protecting your skin from the sun.

If your moisturizer does not have SPF, make sure to apply some! I encourage you to use a mineral sunscreen such as zinc oxide or titanium oxide. These are gentle on the skin and much less toxic compared to chemical sunscreens.

OK. That was a bunch of information. Let's recap and break this down into some fast, frugal options.

1.) Cleanse. At night, wash twice to get all the oil and makeup off.
2.) Exfoliate. If you don't have time to do this every day, once a week will suffice. My recommendation is an electric exfoliating brush. Too expensive? Look up a DIY exfoliation recipe on Pinterest.
3.) If you choose to use a toner, save time by using one that sprays on.
4.) Serum. Consider this more of a luxury item. You'll see great results fast, but this is also optional if you are strapped for time and money.
5.) Moisturize if you have dry skin. Save time by finding one that has a serum in it as well as an SPF. Three steps in one save time!
6.) Apply sunscreen only if your moisturizer doesn't have it already.

So there you have it. This list can easily be broken down and extremely condensed depending on your schedule.

You got this, mama.

5

Body Skin Care

Did your skin change after pregnancy? Yeah. Me too. Postpartum, my skin became very dry on my lips, hands, and legs. If hormonal changes weren't enough, add frequent hand washing from all the diaper changes, bottle washing, and baby bathing, and we have the ideal combination for flaky, cracking fingers. Not only is it unpleasant, but nothing is more frustrating than touching my sweet soft baby with my rough dry hands.

When it comes to skin care from the neck downward, having a high-quality body and hand lotion is something I don't skimp out on. A rich moisturizing cream lotion is ideal for those workin' mama hands. Since I apply lotion upwards of a dozen times a day (sometimes more), and since skin is the largest organ of our body, I prefer a product that is naturally derived. I recommend something free from dyes, parabens, phthalates, and scented only with real essential oils. Brands like Young Living, and 100% Pure are some of my constant go-tos. Keep the lotion by the sink so you can quickly apply after hand washing.

If you're still struggling with rough hands and fingers, my extreme emergency remedy is to apply Vaseline and cover them up with cotton socks before bed (like mittens). A little crazy, but it works. Granted, if you have babies that wake in the middle of the night, you probably won't be able to use this treatment all night, but that's ok! Just an hour or two of this while you sleep can help that skin heal.

As far as the rest of body skin care goes, exfoliating in the shower every now and then is a must. Getting rid of those rough dry skin cells on the top layer of skin will reveal newer, smoother skin that's ready to drink up that moisturizing lotion. You can make your own inexpensive body scrub by simple combining sugar, coconut oil, and lavender essential oil. Do not use salt, as this will be too drying on already dry skin.

Sunless Tanning: Now hear me out... Sunless tanning has come a LONG way since the orange oompa loompa years of the early 2000's. Sunless tanning can be a great way to have a fresh look without spending hours laying in the sun or in a tanning bed (and let's face it, what mama has time for that), but most importantly, you will be reducing your risk of sun damage and skin cancer. I used to love tanning in my 20's, but now that I'm in my 30's, I am reaping the consequences of sun damage. It's just not worth it, mama.

I don't know about you, but when I'm sleep deprived, I start looking sickly and ghostly pale. As mentioned earlier in this book, it all goes back to the lack of blood flow from shallow breathing. We don't realize it, but our poor bodies are actually too tired to breathe correctly! Please note that sunless tanning should not replace the fact that we should sleep, eat well, and exercise in order to get healthy color back to our skin, but if you have family pictures this weekend and you don't want to look like a zombie, this can definitely help. There are plenty of easy-to-apply organic sunless tan lotions out there today. I suggest the following guidelines for a perfect faux glow:

1.) Apply at night after babies go to bed. Sunless tan needs a few hours without water contact to "set". Applying during the day then having to take care of littles with all the splatters and hand washing can lead to disastrous (or humorous) results.

2.) Before applying, take a shower and exfoliate. There's nothing yukkier than having splotchy sunless tan on dry flaky skin.
3.) Use a sunless tanning glove or mit. This will help the product spread evenly onto your body and keep your palms from becoming discolored.
4.) Wear old dark clothes for a few hours after applying.

Note: I do NOT recommend applying anything on your nipples/breasts if you are breastfeeding. Even if the product is safe and organic, it is not something that is intended to be ingested by your baby.

On that same note, here is a time saving tip: It may sound silly, but you don't have to do your entire body! Just apply the lotion to the parts of your body that show. If it's winter and you won't be wearing shorts anytime soon, just apply from the ankles down. If you are wearing a short sleeve shirt, apply from the shoulders and down the arm. (Don't forget your neck and face!) Just wear clothes that cover the pale parts. Keep in mind that sunless tan can last a few days, so be prepared to dress accordingly. Other than your husband, who's probably snickering as he sees you get dressed, who's to know? #sorrynotsorry

6

Hair

I cringe whenever I think about washing my hair. It's a chore. It's hard to get all the shampoo spread evenly throughout my thick hair and scalp, and it takes forever to dry. However, once the task is done, I feel so fresh, renewed, and pretty. It's quite the paradox.

I'll be honest, I've always kept my hair as low maintenance as possible. Since becoming a mommy, styling, and dying has become even less of a priority. I'm sure I'm not the only mama out there that is thankful to simply get a quick hot shower – let's not complicate the morning routine by adding tons of product and curlers.

If you're one of those mamas that prefers styled hair, go for it! There is nothing wrong with that. I personally, am a brush-the-hair-and-go kinda gal in recent days.

Now that I'm in my mid-30's, I see gray. A lot of gray. Not the kind that's hidden either. The kind that's on the top of my scalp. Frizzy. Wiry. In full view. And ya know what? I'm embracing it. I used to be so self-conscious, but I find embracing it to be very freeing. I'm saving so much time and money by just going au naturel. Will I dye my hair again? Like, ever? Sure. I probably will. Just not now. I'd much rather save the money and use that time to snuggle my baby.

It's ok to free yourself of these beauty standards that we all seem to place on ourselves.

I have the same mindset when it comes to styling. I still style my hair every now and then, but for the most part, this is another area that I've embraced going natural.

Just keep it basic, girl. Wash your hair when you need to. As long as you look and feel clean, that's all that matters. Dry shampoo is the best mama invention ever – use it! In fact, medical experts recommend NOT washing your hair every day as this can dry out your scalp and hair. If you have a super oily scalp, extremely fine hair, or if you sweat a lot, you may not be able to get away with prolonging a wash, but I encourage you to keep your routine as easy as possible so you can focus on your babies.

The following is a simple routine I've adapted. I understand that everyone has different hair types and needs, but I'm hoping that sharing my routine will help and inspire other mamas to simplify their own hair regimen:

1.) Wash & condition.
2.) Blow dry at the roots with a round brush. Let the rest air dry.
3.) To control any newly washed hair frizz, spray a leave in conditioner or apply hair oil from mid-hair down to the ends.
4.) Brush hair.
5.) Grab your coffee and go, girl.

If you need to get that hair out of the way for practical workin' mama reasons, throw your hair up in a stylish clip, or dress up that messy top bun with a ribbon or scarf.

On the rare occasion I have some spare time, or want to feel gussied up, I'll spritz a heat activated style spray on my ends and curl my hair with a hot curling wand. I like to do a quick "beach wave" curl and finish with hair spray. Lastly, I'll tease a little on my roots to add a little volume (former pageant girl here, don't judge). This style will last me a few days. If you can find a style that will last you a day or two, this will help you save a huge amount of time while feeling done up. YouTube and Pinterest are full of ideas that can help busy mamas like us. Simply type in "multi day hair" in the search and enjoy. You're welcome.

7

Makeup

Oh, how I love makeup. Makeup and I go way back. My first memory of it goes back to when I was approximately 4 years old. My mom had a glossy black eyeshadow palette filled with frosty blues, purples, and pinks that were the trés chic colors of the late 80's. The smell of the eyeshadow pigment and the protective black velvet bag the case slipped into all brought fascination and joy to my little heart. I played with it. I couldn't help it! I would be suspiciously quiet during this time, and my mom much to her dismay, would discover me. Needless to say, a time out would immediately follow. However, that did not deter my strong-willed little self. Next time mom wasn't looking, I went right back to play with it again.

I still have that makeup palette.

I'm sure it's no surprise that my love of makeup only grew from there. I went on to have a career in makeup and skin care. In addition to my modeling, pageants, and acting, I earned a degree in Theatre with a focus on special effects and stage makeup. I also had the privilege of doing makeup for independent films in Chicago, and worked for major makeup and skin care lines in my current home state of Florida. Today, I assist in helping brides and bridesmaids look amazing for their beach weddings.

Makeup is a big part of my life, so I can't help but continue to have the desire to use it on myself every chance I get, even as a tired mommy. As mentioned earlier, I'm one of those crazy mamas that tries (keyword try) to wake up before baby so I can put myself together for the day – even just a little. It's amazing how much you can accomplish with a cup of coffee and a coat of mascara.

So here are my fast and frugal makeup tips for busy mamas:

Face: If you wear any foundation, is the one makeup product I cannot go cheap on. You get what you pay for. Having a quality foundation will look and feel natural. Sorry, ladies, in my experience, no drugstore foundations have sufficed in my experience. Purchasing better quality foundation will usually mean less breakouts as well. Cheap foundations have synthetic pore clogging ingredients. Just like cleansers, you'll need to find a foundation that suits your skin type. If you have oily skin, you'll need a foundation that's designed for that (or something matte). As a person with dry skin, I need something moisturizing and dewy. I know there are thousands, if not millions of foundation products on the market. Being in the makeup industry, I've tried hundreds myself, and I can say with confidence, that my tried-and-true favorite brands are Clinique, Lancôme, Juice Beauty, Young Living, and HD Makeup Forever. I know I just listed of a lot there, so don't be afraid to walk into a makeup specialty store or department store and ask for help. Unlike drug stores, you can try on foundation and test colors before you buy anything. If you are still unsure, you can request a sample. This will save you so much time and money in the long run because you won't be spending all that cash on finding a good texture and color on cheap drug store foundations.

Nothing is more frustrating to me than standing in a grocery store aisle debating for 15 minutes on whether "Cream" or "Ivory" is the color I need, then getting home and realizing not only that is the color slightly off, but texture cakes, settles into my creases, and clogs my pores. Blah.

Go for high quality and try it on first.

In addition to foundation, I love adding a bit of bronzer. Bronzer allows you to have a little contour without actually putting in the work of contouring. Get the biggest, fluffiest brush you can find and lightly swirl a bit on the top of your forehead (where the sun hits), continue lightly swirling on your cheek bones. Finish it off with pink blush on the apple of your cheeks. Voila! An instant healthy glow with a slight contour effect.

Eyes: Stick with neutrals - something quick and easy. I find that colors in the range of chocolates and taupes look good on nearly every skin tone. I also find that pinks can be a nice option as well (one of my favorites for myself). Don't worry about using all these elaborate pallets with 20 different colors to make the perfect day time eye look like you see on YouTube. Who has time for that?! Get one neutral color. You heard me. One. Then get one small fluffy eyeshadow brush. Apply the eyeshadow with the most pigment and the most pressure on the outside corner of your eye and gently blend inward on your crease with lighter pressure as you move toward the inner corner of your eye. Avoid the eyebrow bone. This will create a beautiful but crazy quick gradient effect that will make it look like you have multiple colors and spent twice as much time on the look. Take the same brush and add a little to your bottom lash line. Add a coat of mascara. Eyeliner on the top lash line is an option if you're feeling extra.

Another great option is lash extensions. I cannot personally attest to this, but plenty of my friends and clients rave about these. If you have the extra cash, it may be worth giving it a try to save you time in the morning. Most women I know that have lash extensions don't apply any makeup. They just let their lashes do the talking. Lashes can last up to 3 weeks if they are done correctly by a licensed professional.

If you are using concealer, try to use something moisturizing and lightweight. Caking on heavy, thick concealer on tired eyes can sometimes make us look worse. If you are using heavier coverage for those mama dark circles, dab on a little moisturizer or eye cream first to help the concealer spread evenly and prevent that textured caked-on look.

Lastly, if you are so sleep deprived that you have blood shot eyes, use some eye drops to freshen up your eyes and brighten your face. I don't recommend doing this every day, but if you need a little extra help, this can really liven up your appearance.

Eyebrows: Most women have their "thing" that they just can't leave the house without. For me, this is my "thing". I'm a brunette that has the unfortunate displeasure of possessing very light, almost blonde, eyebrows and eyelashes. I can't leave the house without eyebrows. I just look silly. Thankfully, there are plenty of inexpensive eyebrow kits or pencils you can purchase at your local drugstore. Dark brown eyeshadow and an angled brush will also give you fast, beautiful results. Use light short strokes when applying and build your way up from there. It's so easy to go too dark or too thick with brows. Short light strokes will keep everything looking natural vs. painted on. A more permanent and time saving option is a relatively new thing called microblading. It's not cheap, but it can save you a huge amount of time in the morning. If you are considering this option proceed with caution. This is just like a tattoo, and it will be on your face for about 2 years. Make sure you weigh all the risks along with the pros and cons. Also make sure go to a licensed professional with plenty of experience.

Lips: Let's be real. I think most mamas are in the same boat when I say the only time I wear lipstick or gloss is for work or a special event. The rest of the time I wear a lip balm with all natural ingredients and essential oils. Then I spend the rest of the day kissing my baby's sweet soft cheeks.

Now that we have all these lovely tips, we just need the time to do it. I'm completely aware that we mamas simply cannot apply all of this makeup every single morning - no matter how fast the application. In the next chapter, I'll be going over quick morning routines you can implement based on the amount of time you have for that particular day.

Let's go, mama!

8

Morning Routine

Ok, mama. This chapter is all about the morning routine. You may love all the tips and tricks in this book, but it won't mean anything if you don't have time to do it! I think you will like this chapter because it breaks everything down into bite sized sections to feel fresh and look lively depending on how schedule crunched your morning is.

The following routines are based on the assumption that you've already done the basic necessities such as shower, brush your teeth, deodorant etc. Yes, there will be some days that showering and brushing your teeth is all you have time to do (sometimes we can't even squeeze THAT in), and that's ok! You're doing great, mama. You're doing great.

Routine #1 - No time:

It's ok, mama! Go hug your babies. There's always tomorrow.

Routine #2 – 1 minute:

Apply moisturizer with SPF, and lip balm.

Routine #3 – 3 minutes:

Moisturizer with SPF, eye cream, and lip balm.

Routine #4 – 6 minutes:

Moisturizer with SPF, eye cream, lip balm, fill in eyebrows and add mascara on top lash.

Routine #5 – 8 minutes:
Moisturizer with SPF, eye cream, lip balm, eyebrows, one neutral eyeshadow color, mascara on top lash.

Routine #6 – 10 minutes:
Moisturizer with SPF, eye cream, lip balm, eyebrows, neutral eyeshadow, mascara on top lash, and bronzer.

Routine #7 – 12 minutes: ***My favorite morning routine if time allows***
Moisturizer with SPF, eye cream, lip balm, foundation, eyebrows, neutral eyeshadow, mascara, and bronzer.

Routine #8 – 15+ minutes: ***Routine for getting fancy or going somewhere important – this is usually done when baby is sleeping***
Toner, moisturizer with SPF, eye cream, lip balm, foundation, eyebrows, eyeshadow, eyeliner, mascara, bronzer, blush, lip color.

Add another minute to any routine for a touch of dry shampoo and/or eye drops for bloodshot eyes.

Add another 15 minutes for curling hair.

Now go drink some coffee and have an amazing day, mama.

9

Conclusion

So there you have it. Don't forget- above all, your babies come first. They don't care if you have mascara on. They want you. Love them. Snuggle them. Nothing makes my cup of joy overflow more than picking up my sweet soft baby in the morning light. His cheeks are pink from a warm heavy sleep, and his fuzzy hair sticks out every direction. He stretches, wiggles in my arms, and coos contently. I can't help but kiss his baby round cheeks repeatedly. In moments like that, I'm not thinking about eye cream or makeup. Neither is my baby.

We mamas just gotta make sure we are well enough mentally, emotionally, and physically to take care of our littles. Everything else can wait. From what I hear, despite the extreme fatigue, sometime in the not-so-distant future, we will miss these days.

As long as you are taking care of your babies, that's all matters. THAT is beautiful, mama.

10

Resources

Austen, A. (2021, September 10). *Understanding The Difference Between Facial And Body Skin*. The Beauty Chef. Retrieved October 2, 2022, from https://thebeautychef.com/blogs/blog/understanding-the-difference-between-facial-and-body-skin#:%7E:text=The%20main%20differences%20between%20facial,the%20body%20than%20the%20face.

Bilodeau, K. (2018, June 12). *Skin serum: What it can and can't do*. Harvard Health. Retrieved October 2, 2022, from https://www.health.harvard.edu/blog/skin-serum-what-it-can-and-cant-do-2018061214029#:%7E:text=Serums%20are%20light%2C%20easily%20absorbed,lotion%20or%20cream%2C%20says%20Dr.

Cardellino, C. (2015, July 21). *8 Ways Too Little Sleep Can Mess With Your Face*. Cosmopolitan. Retrieved October 2, 2022, from https://www.cosmopolitan.com/style-beauty/beauty/advice/a42908/ways-sleep-can-mess-with-your-face/

Contributed by Zawn Villines, GoodTherapy.org Correspondent. (2017, January 5). *Effective Goal Setting Could Help People with Depression.*

GoodTherapy.org Therapy Blog. Retrieved October 2, 2022, from https://www.goodtherapy.org/blog/effective-goal-setting-could-h elp-people-with-depression-0105171#:%7E:text=Although%20lack% 20of%20motivation%20often,they%20could%20achieve%20their%20 goals.

Cutting back on sleep harms blood vessel function and breathing control. (n.d.). ScienceDaily. Retrieved October 2, 2022, from https://www.scien cedaily.com/releases/2013/04/130422102026.htm#:%7E:text=Summar y%3A,function%20and%20impaired%20breathing%20control.

Fleur & Bee. (n.d.). *Facial Toner: 5 Benefits and Why You Should Use it.* Fleur & Bee. Retrieved October 2, 2022, from https://fleurandbee.com/b logs/news/benefits-of-facial-toner#:%7E:text=In%20a%20nutshell% 2C%20toners%20are,naturally%20remove%20oil%20and%20dirt.

How Often Should You Wash Your Hair? (2011, September 21). WebMD. Retrieved October 2, 2022, from https://www.webmd.com/beauty/featu res/how-often-wash-hair#:%7E:text=Who%20Should%20Shampoo% 20Daily%3F,is%20needed%2C%E2%80%9D%20she%20explains.

Lane, D. (2016, June 3). *The Many Ways Cheap Makeup Is Aging Your Skin - BlackDoctor.org - Where Wellness & Culture Connect.* BlackDoctor.org. Retrieved October 2, 2022, from https://blackdoctor.org/the-many-wa ys-cheap-makeup-is-aging-your-skin/

McCallum. (2022, May 17). *Mineral Vs. Chemical Sunscreen: Does It Matter Which You Use?* https://www.houstonmethodist.org/blog/articles/2022/ may/mineral-vs-chemical-sunscreen-does-it-matter-which-you-us e/#:~:text=For%20someone%20with%20sensitive%20skin,Sensitive %20skin%2C%22%20explains%20Christenson. https://www.houston

methodist.org/blog/articles/2022/may/mineral-vs-chemical-sunscree
n-does-it-matter-which-you-use/#:~:text=For%20someone%20with
%20sensitive%20skin,sensitive%20skin%2C%22%20explains%20Chr
istenson.

National Heart, Lung & Blood Institutue. (2022, March 24). *Why Is Sleep
Important?* NHLBI, NIH. Retrieved October 2, 2022, from https://www.n
hlbi.nih.gov/health/sleep/why-sleep-important#:%7E:text=During%2
0sleep%2C%20your%20body%20is,long%2Dterm)%20health%20pro
blems.

National Institute of Mental Health. (n.d.). *Caring for your mental health.*
https://www.nimh.nih.gov/health/topics/caring-for-your-mental-hea
lth

Nazish, N. (2021, March 31). *Do You Really Need A Face Toner? Here's What
The Derms Say.* Forbes. Retrieved October 2, 2022, from https://www.for
bes.com/sites/nomanazish/2021/03/31/do-you-really-need-a-face-to
ner-heres-what-the-derms-say/?sh=65b7756f446f

YARBOROUGH. (2017, November 25). *Anxiety, gratitude cannot co-exist.*
The Brunswick News. https://thebrunswicknews.com/life/anxiety-grat
itude-cannot-co-exist/article_4281bf40-671d-5cd7-a18e-43a4ca8c6
ccd.html#:~:text=Research%20shows%20that%20worry%20and,choo
ses%20to%20completely%20take%20over.

About the Author

Meghan has extensive experience in the makeup and skin care world, and she held the title of Miss Jr. South Carolina and 2nd Runner Up for Miss Jr. America in 2005. She is also an experienced actress and model, in addition to a career in the makeup industry. She loves using her knowledge and experience to help people in the realm of beauty and fashion. Meghan is the proud mommy of a sweet baby boy, and lives with her husband, Chris, in Florida.

Printed in Dunstable, United Kingdom